U2 ALL THAT YOU CAN'T
LEAVE BEHIND

Exclusive distributors:
Music Sales Limited
8/9 Frith Street,
London W1D 3JB, England.
Music Sales Pty Limited
120 Rothschild Avenue
Rosebery, NSW 2018,
Australia.

Order No.AM968451
ISBN 0-7119-8635-5
This book © Copyright 2000 by Universal Music Publishing

Music arranged by James Dean
Music engraved by Paul Ewers Music Design
Book design by Shaughn McGrath, Four 5 One Design, Dublin

Printed in the United Kingdom by
Printwise (Haverhill) Limited, Haverhill, Suffolk.

Your Guarantee of Quality
As publishers, we strive to produce every book to the highest commercial standards. The music has been freshly engraved and, whilst endeavouring to retain the original running order of the recorded album, the book has been carefully designed to minimise awkward page turns and to make playing from it a real pleasure. Particular care has been given to specifying acid-free, neutral-sized paper made from pulps which have not been elemental chlorine bleached. This pulp is from farmed sustainable forests and was produced with special regard for the environment. Throughout, the printing and binding have been planned to ensure a sturdy, attractive publication which should give years of enjoyment. If your copy fails to meet our high standards, please inform us and we will gladly replace it.

www.musicsales.com
www.U2.com

GUITAR TABLATURE EXPLAINED

Guitar music can be notated three different ways: on a musical stave, in tablature, and in rhythm slashes

RHYTHM SLASHES are written above the stave. Strum chords in the rhythm indicated. Round noteheads indicate single notes.

THE MUSICAL STAVE shows pitches and rhythms and is divided by lines into bars. Pitches are named after the first seven letters of the alphabet.

TABLATURE graphically represents the guitar fingerboard. Each horizontal line represents a string, and each number represents a fret.

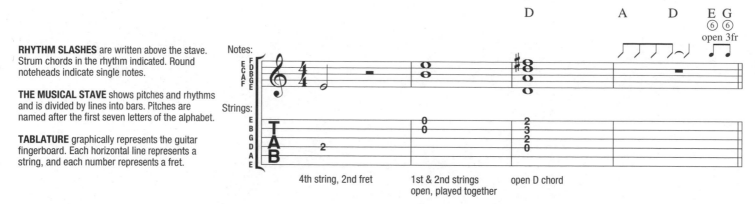

4th string, 2nd fret

1st & 2nd strings open, played together

open D chord

DEFINITIONS FOR SPECIAL GUITAR NOTATION

SEMI-TONE BEND: Strike the note and bend up a semi-tone (1/2 step).

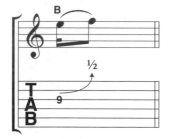

WHOLE-TONE BEND: Strike the note and bend up a whole-tone (whole step).

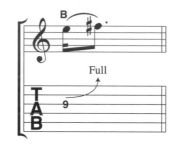

GRACE NOTE BEND: Strike the note and bend as indicated. Play the first note as quickly as possible.

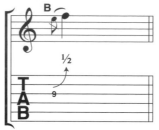

QUARTER-TONE BEND: Strike the note and bend up a 1/4 step.

BEND & RELEASE: Strike the note and bend up as indicated, then release back to the original note.

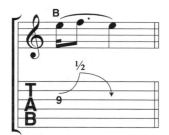

BEND & RESTRIKE: Strike the note and bend as indicated then restrike the string where the symbol occurs.

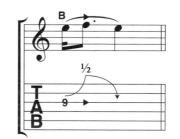

PRE-BEND: Bend the note as indicated, then strike it.

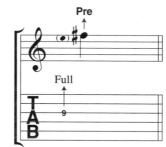

PRE-BEND & RELEASE: Bend the note as indicated. Strike it and release the note back to the original pitch.

HAMMER-ON: Strike the first (lower) note with one finger, then sound the higher note (on the same string) with another finger by fretting it without picking.

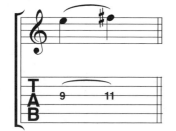

PULL-OFF: Place both fingers on the notes to be sounded. Strike the first note and without picking, pull the finger off to sound the second (lower) note.

LEGATO SLIDE (GLISS): Strike the first note and then slide the same fret-hand finger up or down to the second note. The second note is not struck.

SHIFT SLIDE (GLISS & RESTRIKE): Same as legato slide, except the second note is struck.

NATURAL HARMONIC: Strike the note while the fret-hand lightly touches the string directly over the fret indicated.

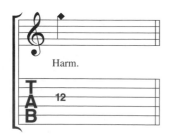

PICK SCRAPE: The edge of the pick is rubbed down (or up) the string, producing a scratchy sound.

PALM MUTING: The note is partially muted by the pick hand lightly touching the string(s) just before the bridge.

MUFFLED STRINGS: A percussive sound is produced by laying the fret hand across the string(s) without depressing, and striking them with the pick hand.

NOTE: The speed of any bend is indicated by the music notation and tempo.

BEAUTIFUL DAY

Music by U2
Lyrics by Bono

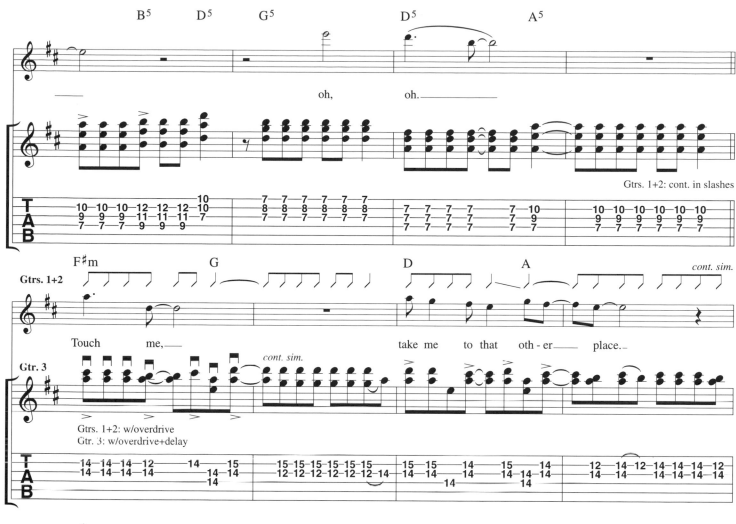

oh,   oh.

Gtrs. 1+2: cont. in slashes

Gtrs. 1+2

Touch   me,——   take me   to that   oth-er——   place.—

Gtr. 3

Gtrs. 1+2: w/overdrive
Gtr. 3: w/overdrive+delay

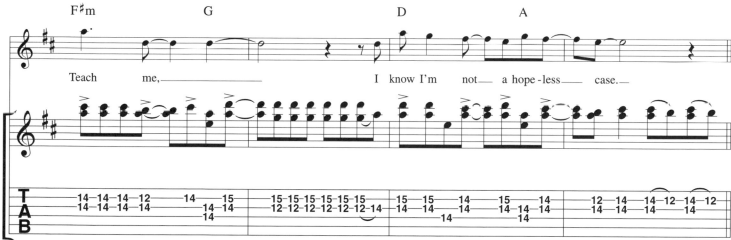

Teach   me,————————   I   know I'm   not— a hope-less—   case.—

Instrumental

Instrumental

(A)   (Bm)   (D)   (G)   (D)   (A)

Gtr. 2

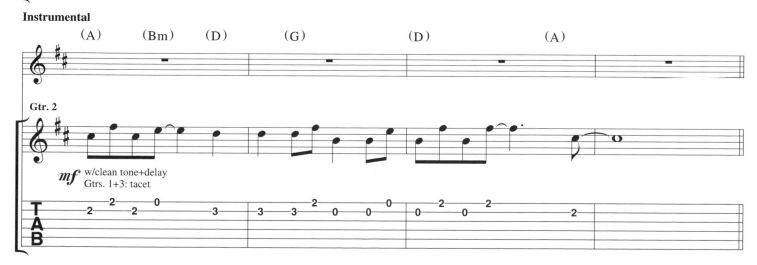

mf w/clean tone+delay
Gtrs. 1+3: tacet

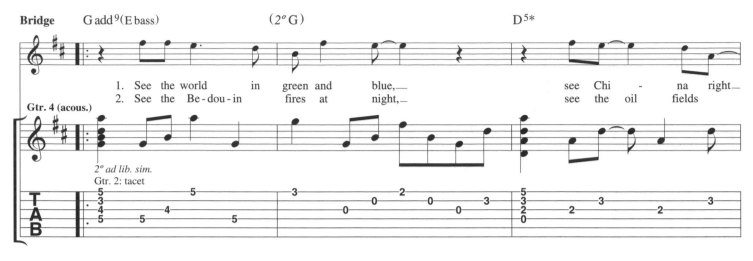

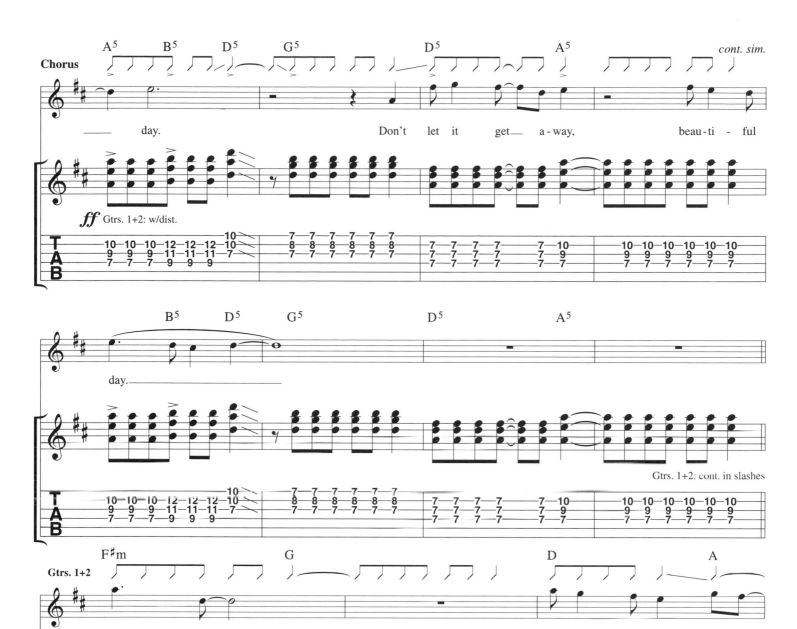

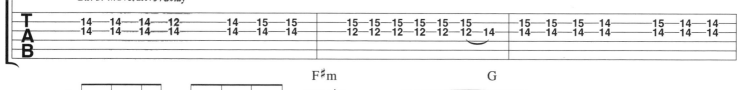

STUCK IN A MOMENT YOU CAN'T GET OUT OF

Music by U2
Lyrics by Bono & The Edge

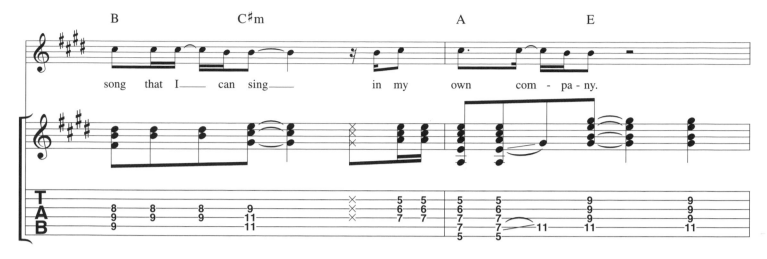

song that I ____ can sing____ in my own com - pa - ny.

I nev - er thought you were a fool, ____

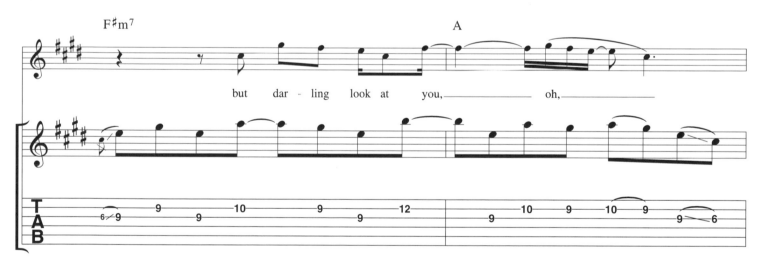

but dar - ling look at you, ____ oh, ____

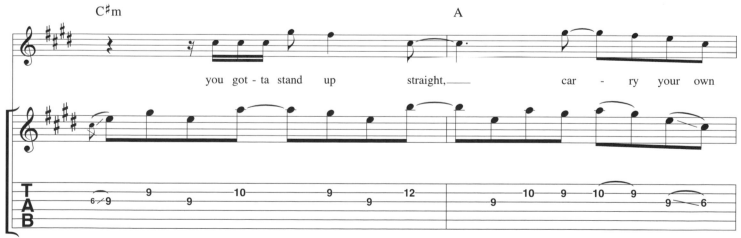

you got - ta stand up straight, ____ car - ry your own

20

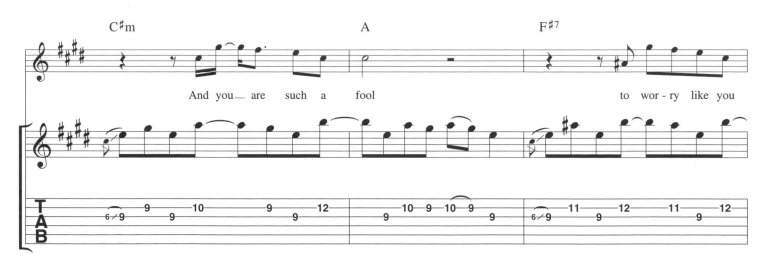

And you— are such a fool to wor-ry like you

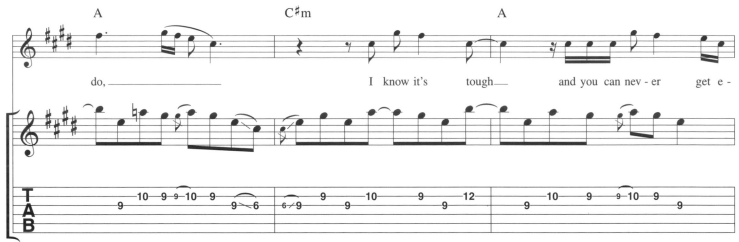

do, _____ I know it's tough— and you can nev-er get e-

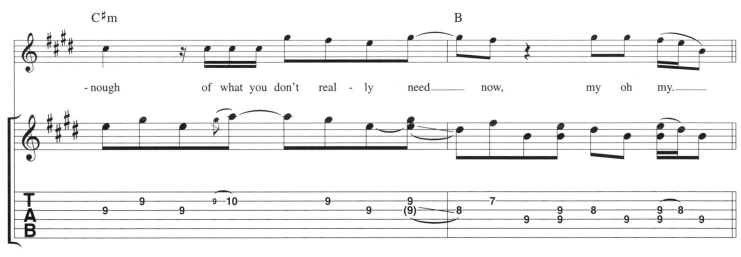

-nough of what you don't real-ly need—— now, my oh my.——

Chorus 𝄊

You've got to get your-self to-geth-er, you've got stuck in a mo-ment, now you

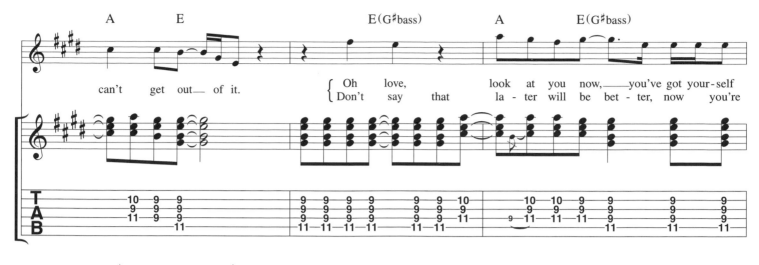

can't get out of it.

{ Oh love, that look at you now,——you've got your-self
{ Don't say that la-ter will be bet-ter, now you're

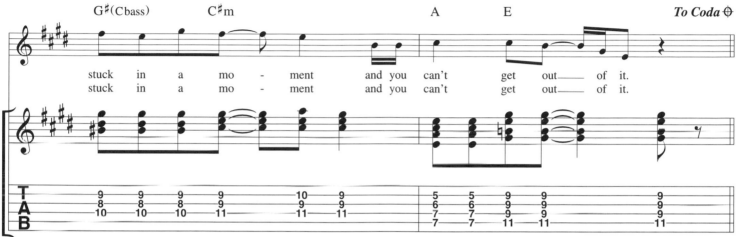

stuck in a mo - ment and you can't get out—— of it.
stuck in a mo - ment and you can't get out—— of it.

To Coda ⊕

Middle F#m A

I was un-con-scious, half—a-sleep, the wa-ter is warm—'til you dis-co-ver—— how deep.—

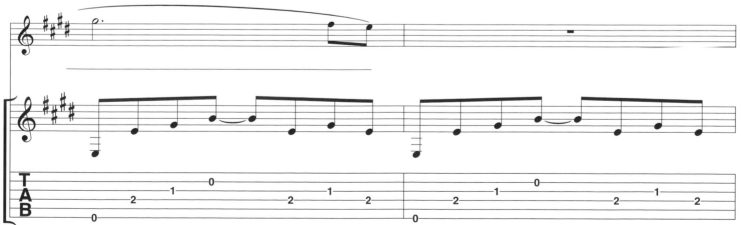

E

24

ELEVATION

Music by U2
Lyrics by Bono

Verse

1. High, high-er than the sun,___ you shoot me from a gun,___ I need you to

Gtr. 1   2. A star, lit up like a ci - gar,___ strung out like a gui - tar,___ may - be you could

Gtr. 2: tacet
Fig. 2

e - le - vate___ me, here.___ At the cor - ner of your lips, as the or - bit of your

e - du - cate___ my mind.___ Ex - plain all these con - trols, (I) can't sing but I've got

hips, ec - lipse, you e - le - - - vate___ my

soul, the goal is e - le - - - va - tion. A

Chorus (B)   (A)   (E)

        soul   I've lost all self - con - trol, been liv - ing like a

2, (%) mole   liv - ing in a hole, dig - ging up my

Gtr. 3 (acous.)

Gtr. 1: w/Fig. 2 (x4)

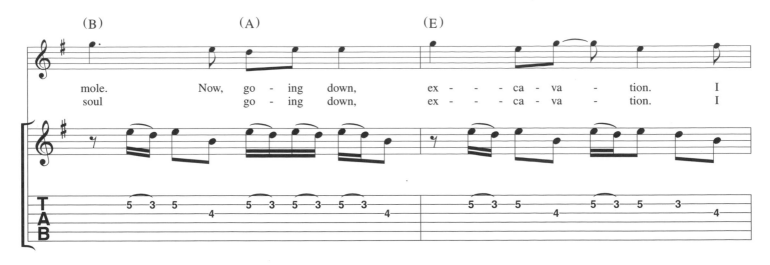

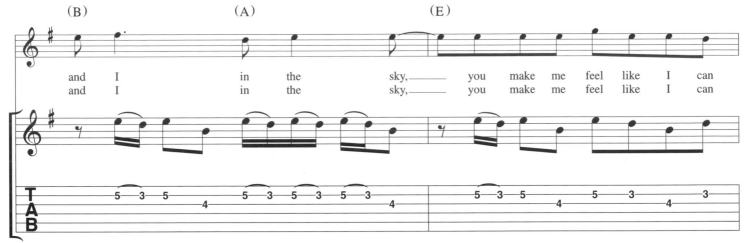

WALK ON

Music by U2
Lyrics by Bono
Dedicated to Aung San Suu Kyi

Verse

1. And if the dark-ness is to keep us a-
2. You're pack-ing a suit-case for a place none of us has

part,
been,

and if the day-light feels like it's
a place that has to be be-lieved

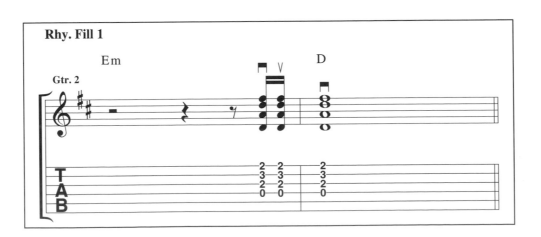

Rhy. Fill 1

they can't ev - en feel it. Walk on,_____ walk on,_____
sell it,___ can't buy it. Walk on,_____ walk on,_____

1.
2.

stay safe to - night._____
stay safe to - night.__

And I know__

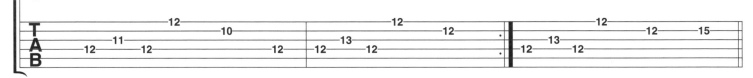

_____ it aches,__ and your heart it breaks, (and) you can on - ly take__ so much.__ Walk

Solo
Gtrs. 2+3

cont. sim.

on.__

Gtr. 4

Gtr. 1: tacet

you've got to leave it be - hind.＿ All that you fash-

- ion,   all that you make,＿   all that you build,＿   all that you break.＿
rea - son,   all that you make,＿   all that you build,＿   all that you break.＿

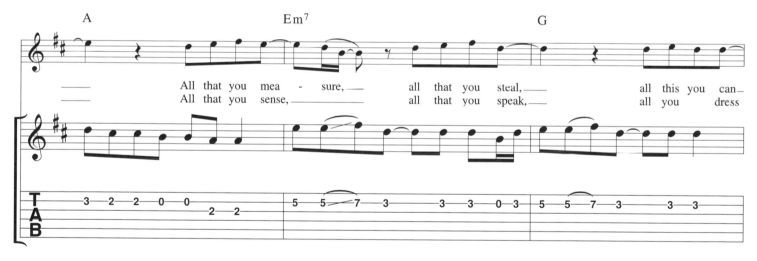

All that you mea - sure,＿   all that you steal,＿   all this you can＿
All that you sense,＿   all that you speak,＿   all you dress

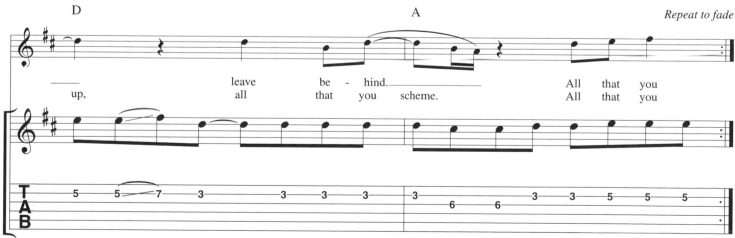

Repeat to fade

up,   leave   be - hind.＿   All   that   you
     all   that   you   scheme.   All   that   you

KITE

Music by U2
Lyrics by Bono & The Edge

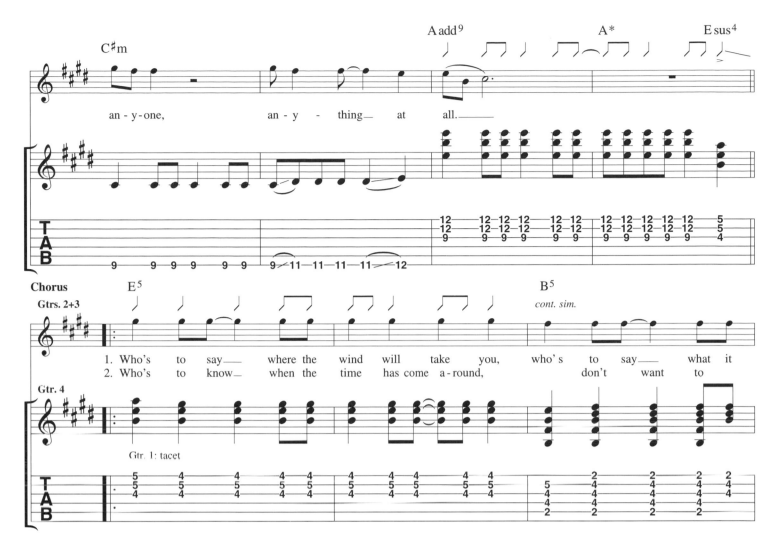

Chorus
Gtrs. 2+3

1. Who's to say where the wind will take you, who's to say what it
2. Who's to know when the time has come a-round, don't want to

Gtr. 4

Gtr. 1: tacet

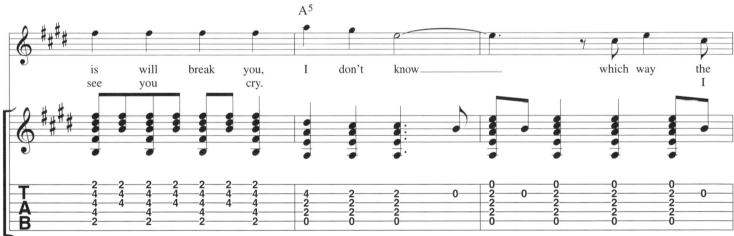

is will break you, I don't know which way the
see you cry. I

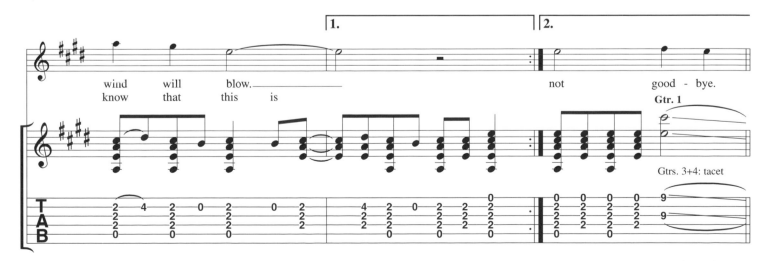

wind will blow. not good-bye.
know that this is

Gtr. 1

Gtrs. 3+4: tacet

won - der what has hap - pened to me._____

Gtr. 4

w/slide

Instrumental A

Gtrs. 2+3 *cont. sim.*

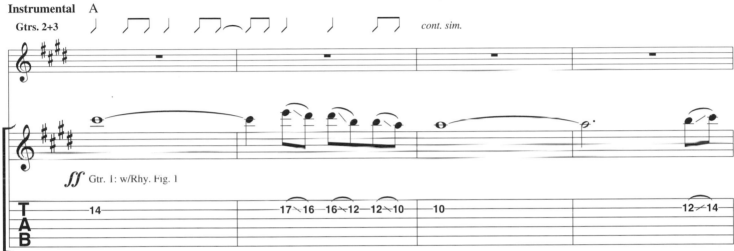

ff Gtr. 1: w/Rhy. Fig. 1

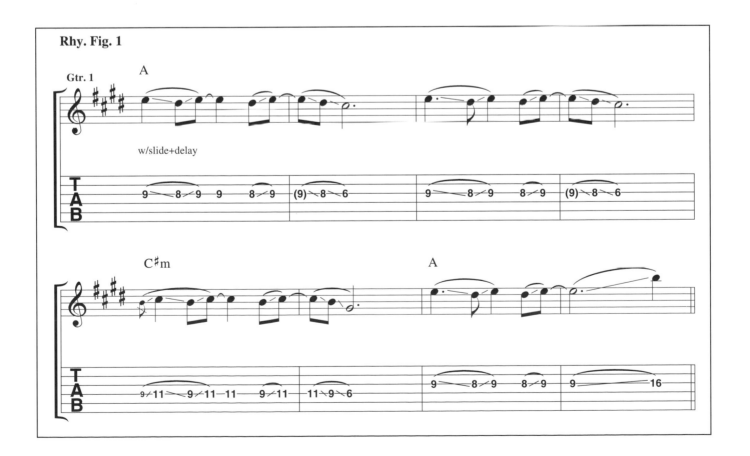

Rhy. Fig. 1

Gtr. 1 A

w/slide+delay

C#m

A

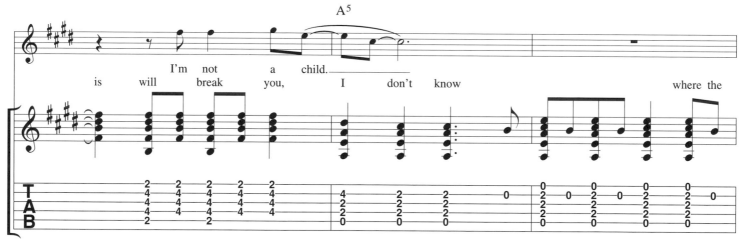

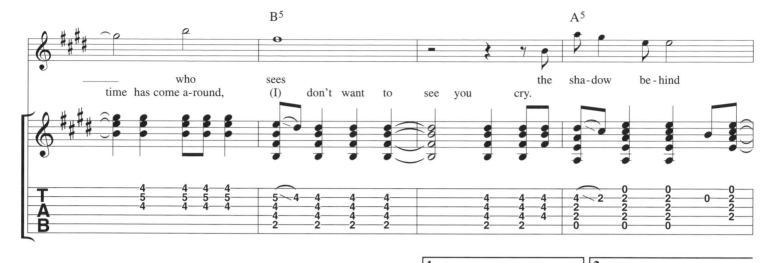

time has come a-round, who sees (I) don't want to the sha-dow be-hind see you cry.

your eyes. I know that this is not good-bye.

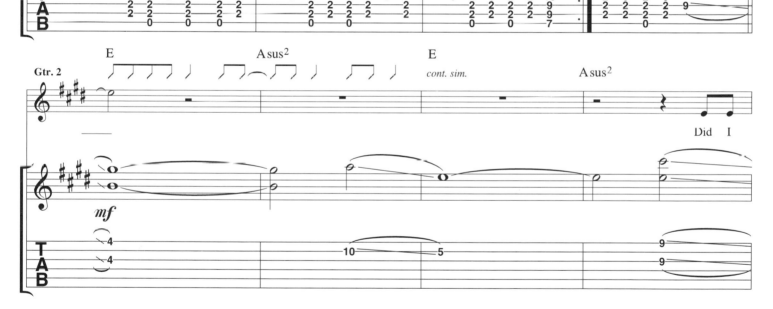

Did I waste it,

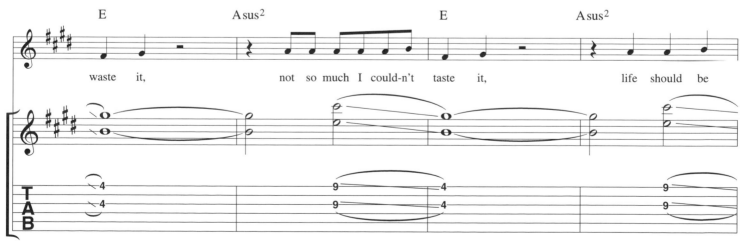

waste it, not so much I could-n't taste it, life should be

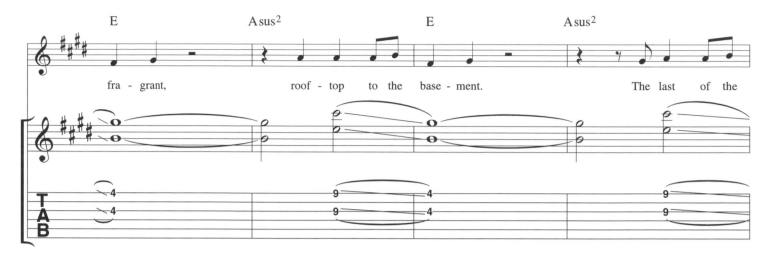

fra - grant, roof - top to the base - ment. The last of the

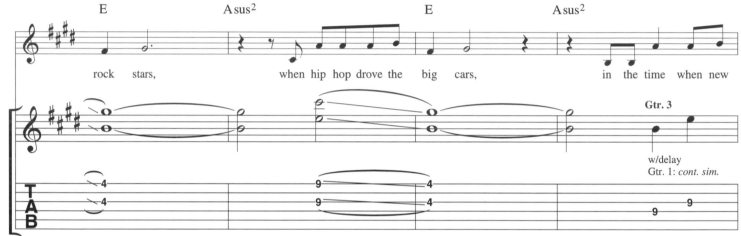

rock stars, when hip hop drove the big cars, in the time when new

Gtr. 3

w/delay
Gtr. 1: *cont. sim.*

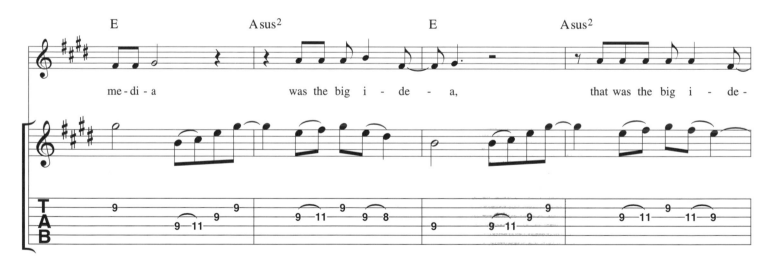

me - di - a was the big i - de - a, that was the big i - de -

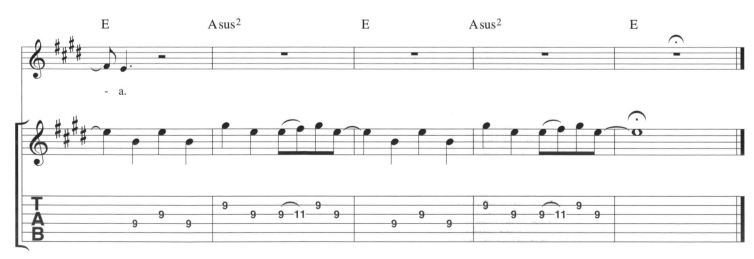

- a.

IN A LITTLE WHILE

Music by U2
Lyrics by Bono

in a lit-tle while I'll be there. In a lit-tle while,— this hurt—
Fri-day night run-ning to Sun-day on my knees. That girl,— that girl,—

...Fig. 1 ends   *2° Gtr. 1: w/Fig. 1 (x2)*

—— will hurt— no more,— I'll be home love. When the night—
—— she's mine,— well I have known her since, since she was a lit-

-tle girl   takes   a deep breath,_____   and the day-light_____   has no   air._____
with   Span - ish eyes.

Play 1° & 2°

_____ pram they pushed her by.   If I   crawl,   if I   come crawl - ing home,_____   will you
Oh   my,   my   how you've grown,   well it's

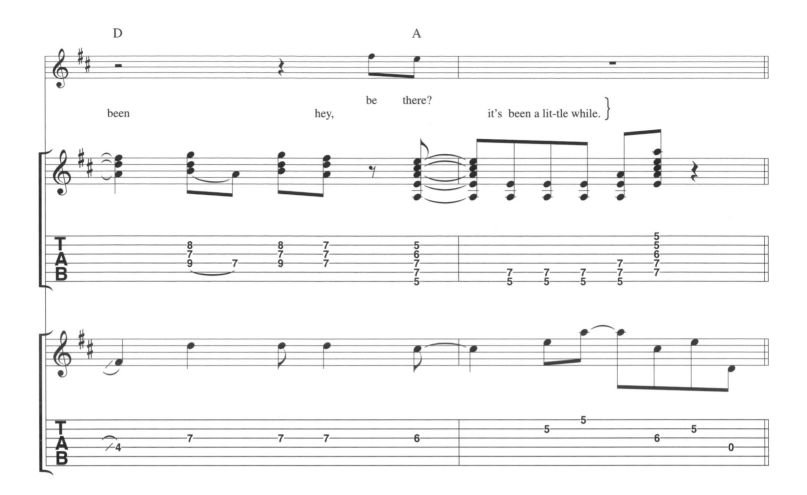

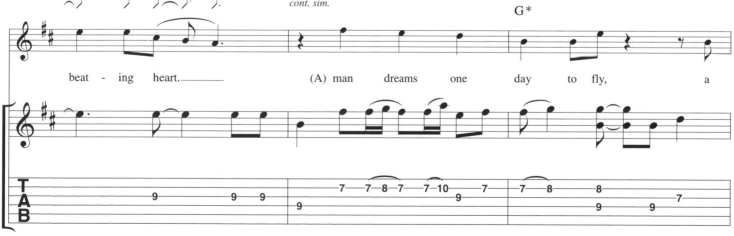

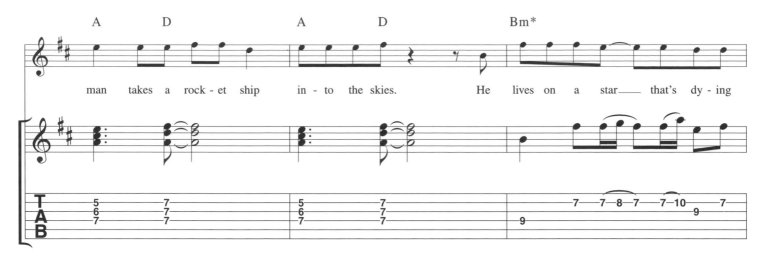

man takes a rock - et ship in - to the skies. He lives on a star that's dy - ing

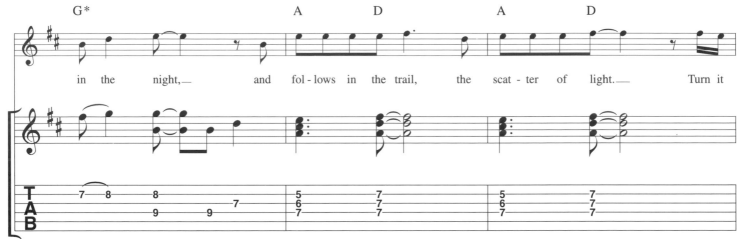

in the night, and fol - lows in the trail, the scat - ter of light. Turn it

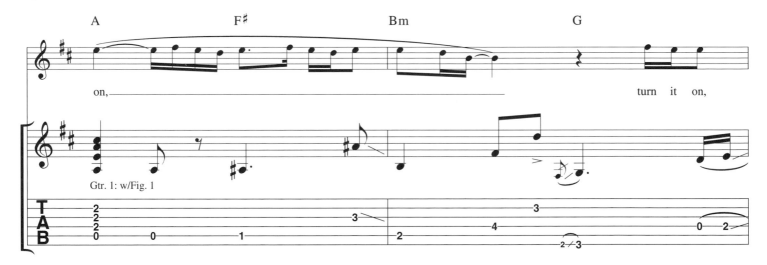

on, turn it on,

Gtr. 1: w/Fig. 1

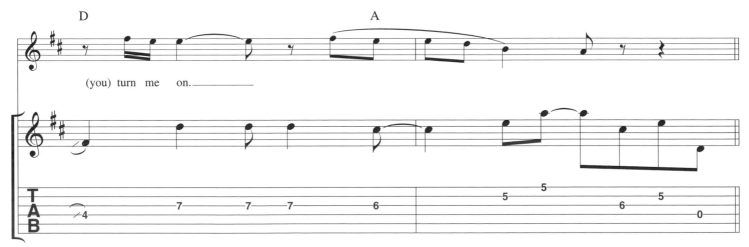

(you) turn me on.

WILD HONEY

Music by U2
Lyrics by Bono

55

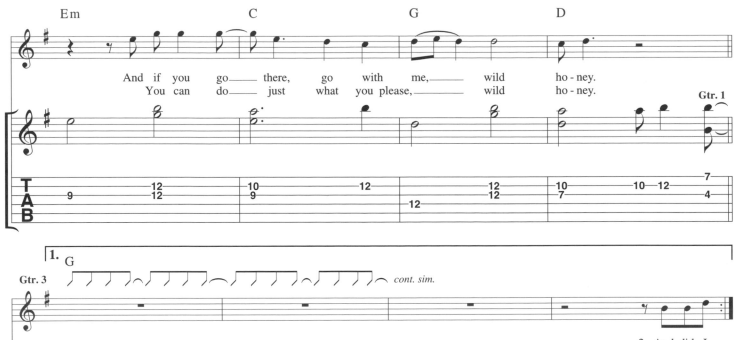

And if you go there, go with me, wild ho-ney.
You can do just what you please, wild ho-ney.

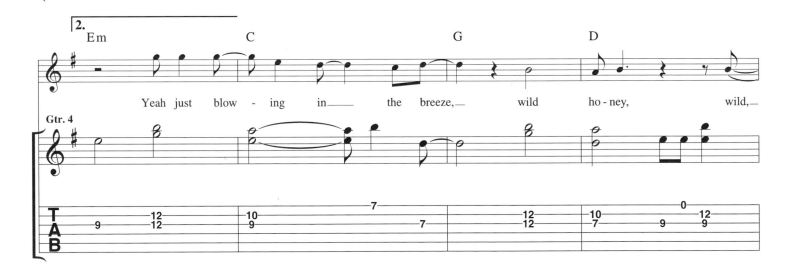

2. And did I

Yeah just blow-ing in the breeze, wild ho-ney, wild,

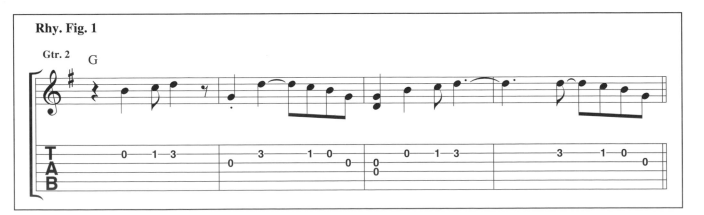

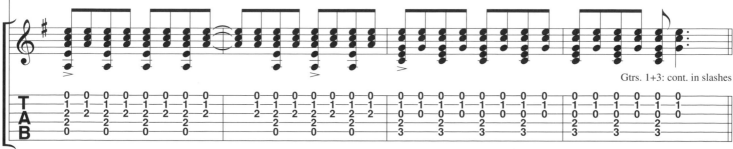

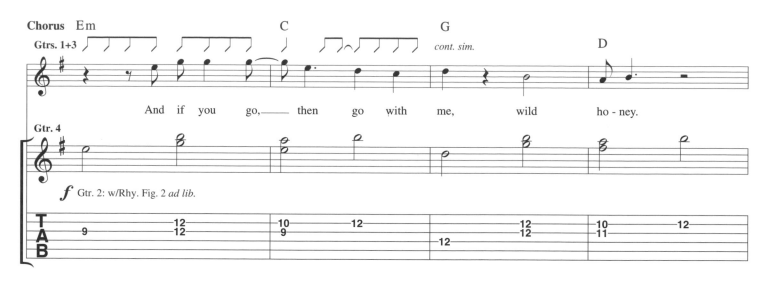

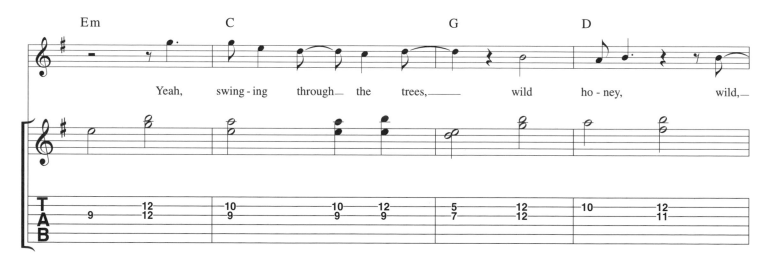

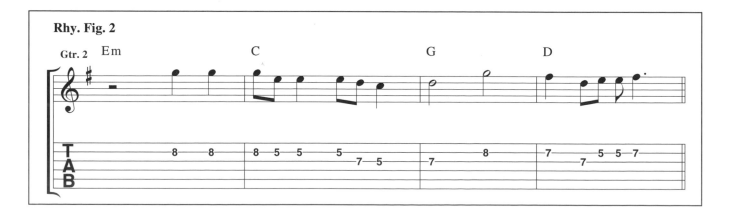

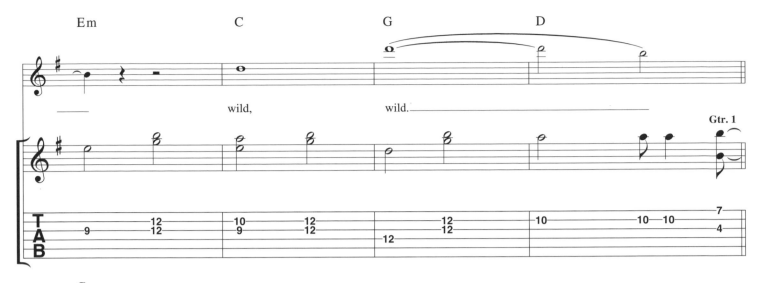

Verse 3 (𝄌):
I'm still standing
I'm still standing where you left me.
Are you still growing wild
With everything tame around you?
I send you flowers
Cut flowers for your hall
I know your garden's full
But is there sweetness at all?

PEACE ON EARTH

Music by U2
Lyrics by Bono

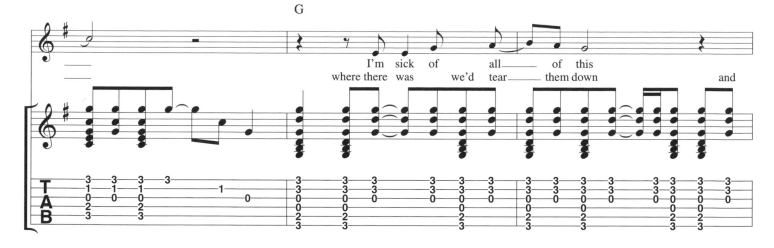

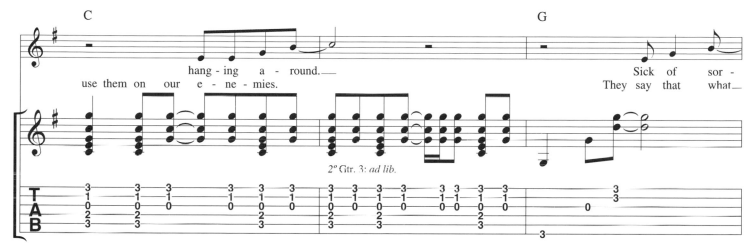

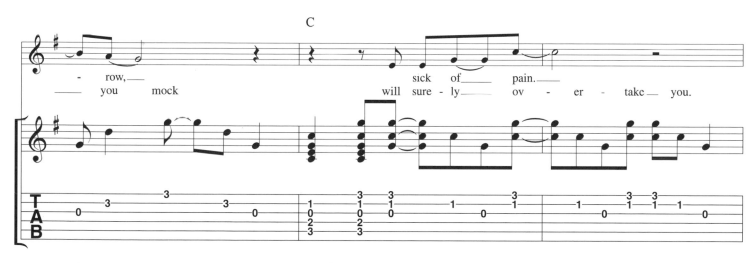

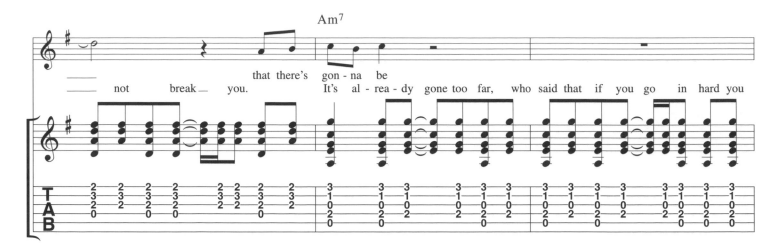

peace on earth.___ No, who's or why's, no one cries like a moth-er cries for

peace on earth.___ She nev - er got to say good-bye, to

see the co - lour in his eyes, now he's in the dirt,___

peace on earth.___

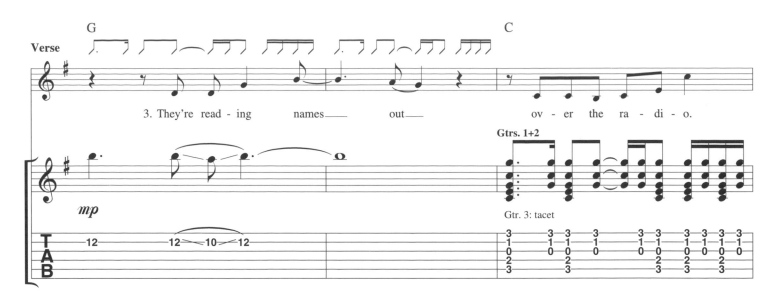

3. They're read-ing names___ out___ ov-er the ra-di-o.

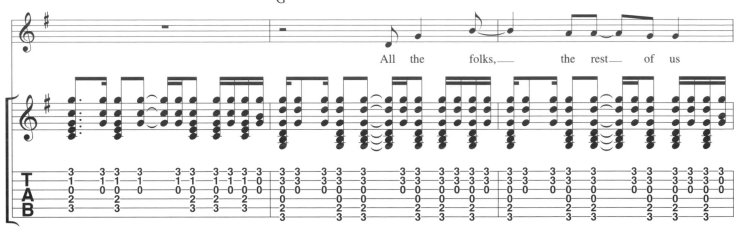

All the folks,___ the rest___ of us

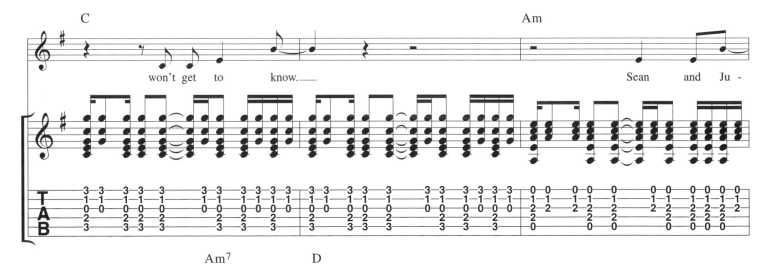

won't get to know.___ Sean and Ju-

-li - a,___ Ga-reth, Ann___ and Bre - da,

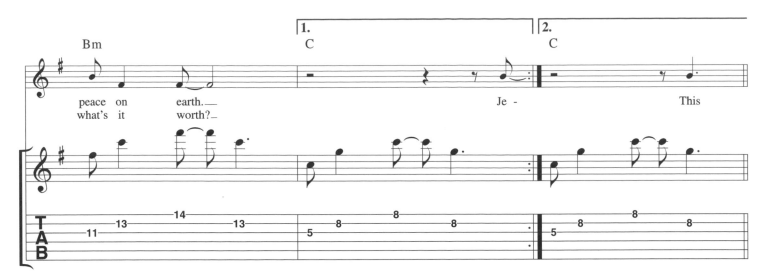

Outro

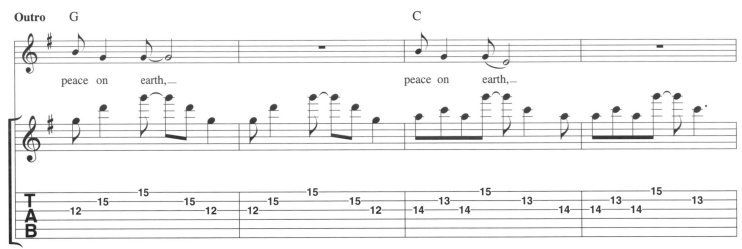

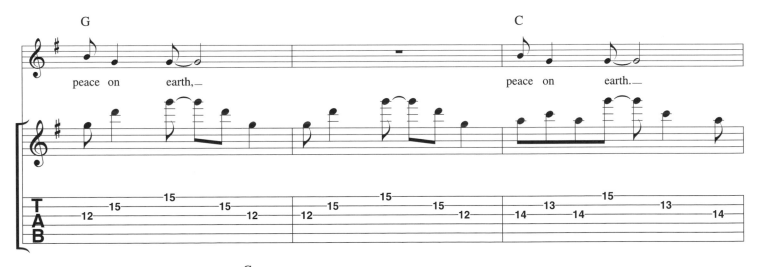

NEW YORK

Music by U2
Lyrics by Bono

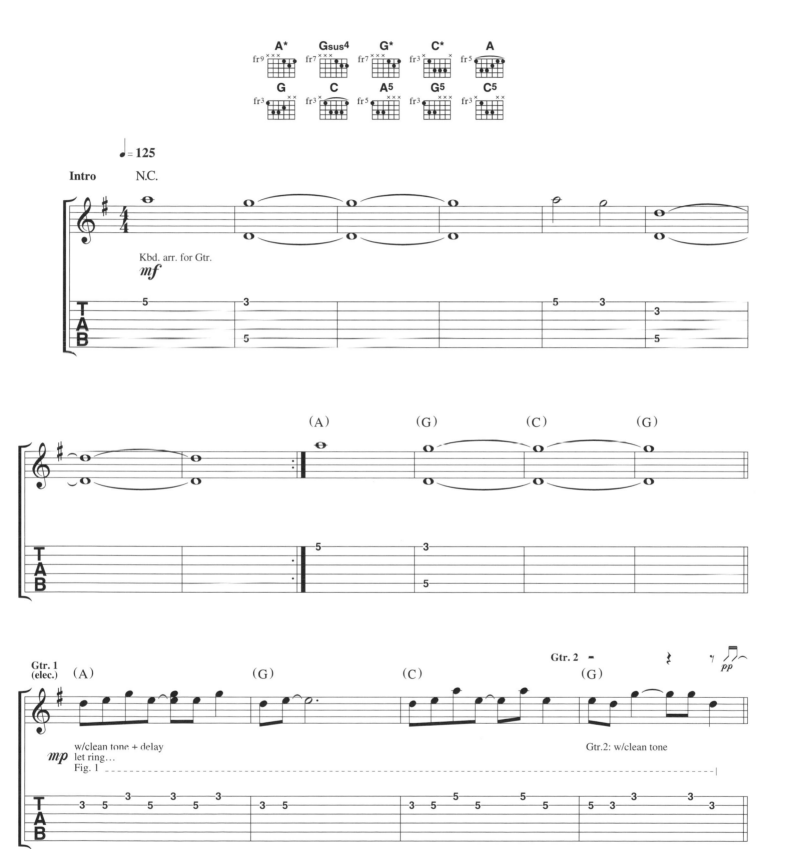

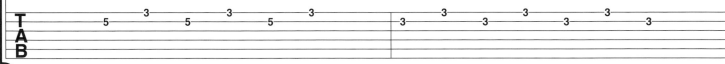

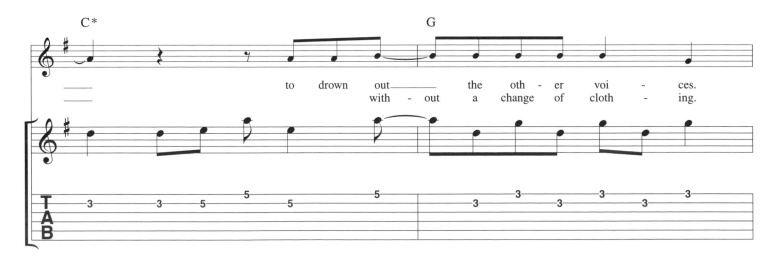

Voi - ces on the cell phone, voi - ces from home, voi - ces of the hard sell, voi - ces down the stair - well, in ___
Hot as a hair - dryer in your face, hot as a hand - bag and a can of mace. In New-

1° Gtr. 2: w/Rhy. Fig. 1

1.

___ New York, just got a place in New York. ___
York, I just got a place in New - York. ___

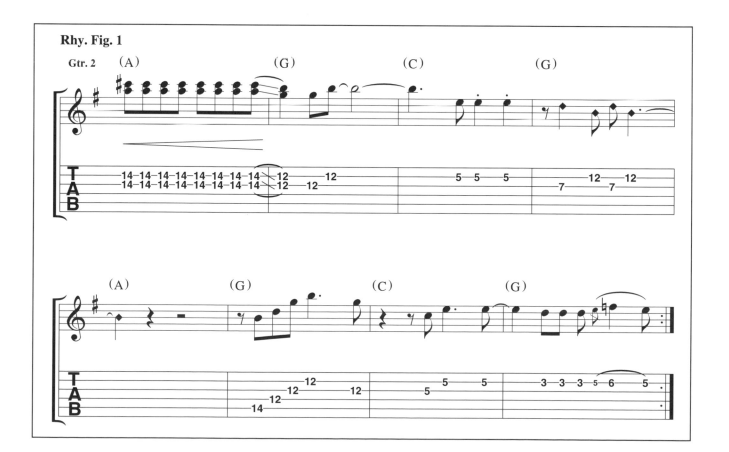

Rhy. Fig. 1

Gtr. 2 (A) (G) (C) (G)

(A) (G) (C) (G)

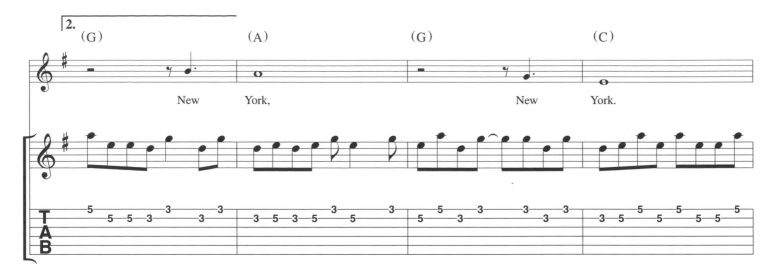

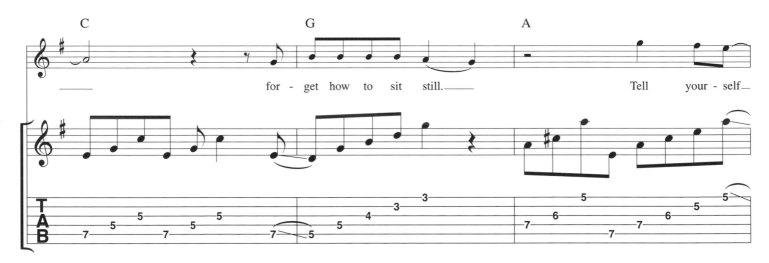

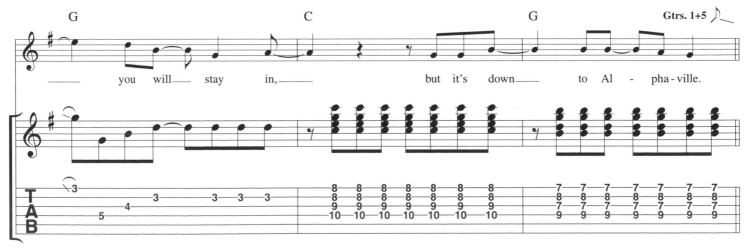

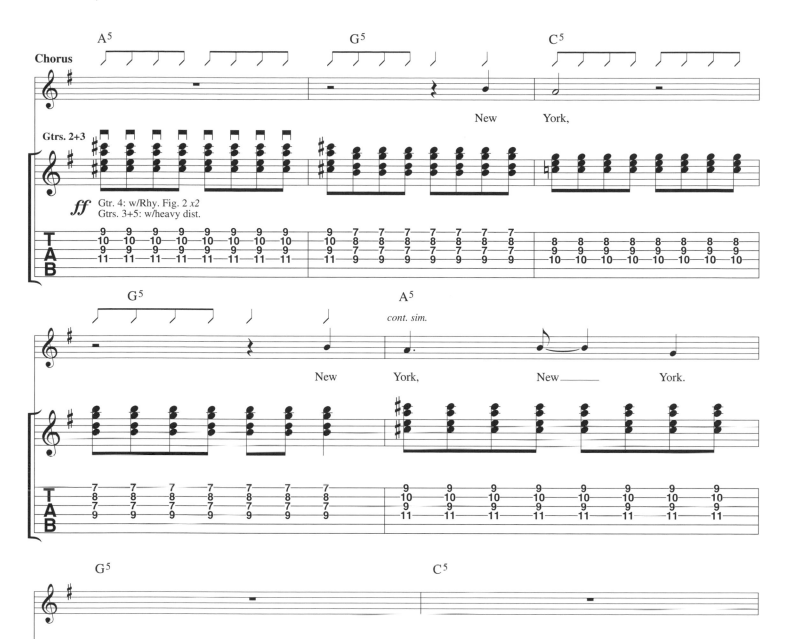

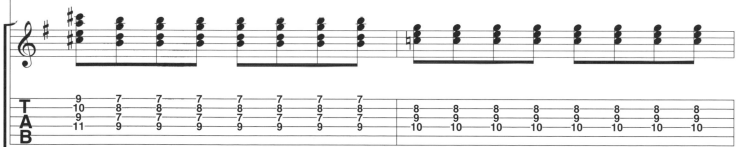

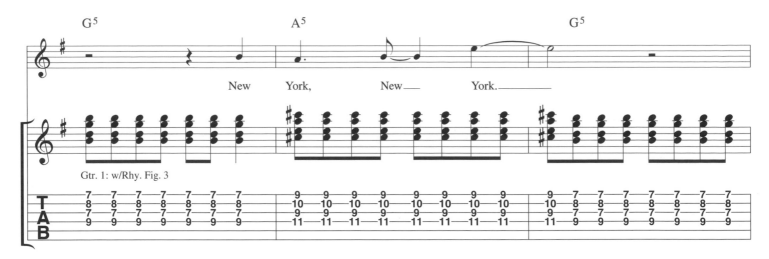

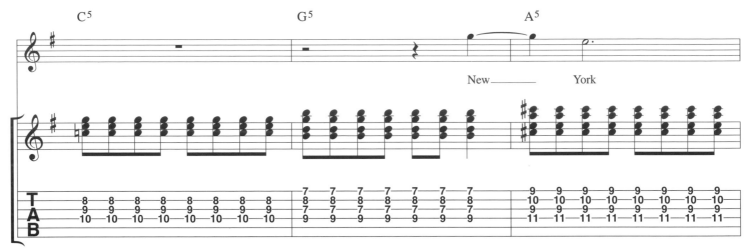

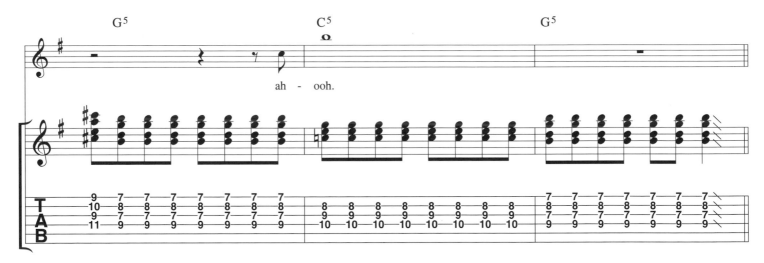

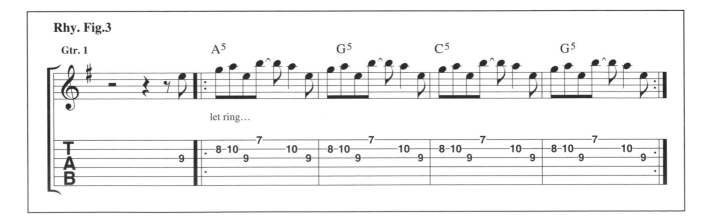

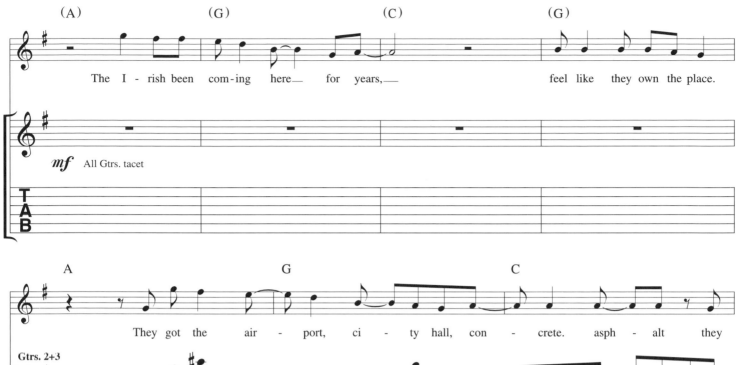

(A) (G) (C) (G)

The I - rish been com-ing here— for years,— feel like they own the place.

mf All Gtrs. tacet

A G C

They got the air - port, ci - ty hall, con - crete. asph - alt they

Gtrs. 2+3

Gtr. 1: w/Fig. 1 *x3 ad lib.*

G A G

ev - en got the po - lice. I - rish, I - ta - li - an, Jews and His - pa - nics, re -

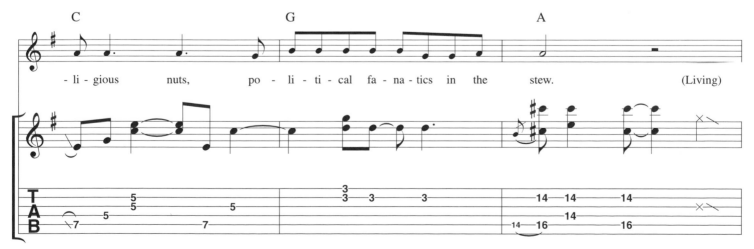

C G A

- li - gious nuts, po - li - ti - cal fa - na - tics in the stew. (Living)

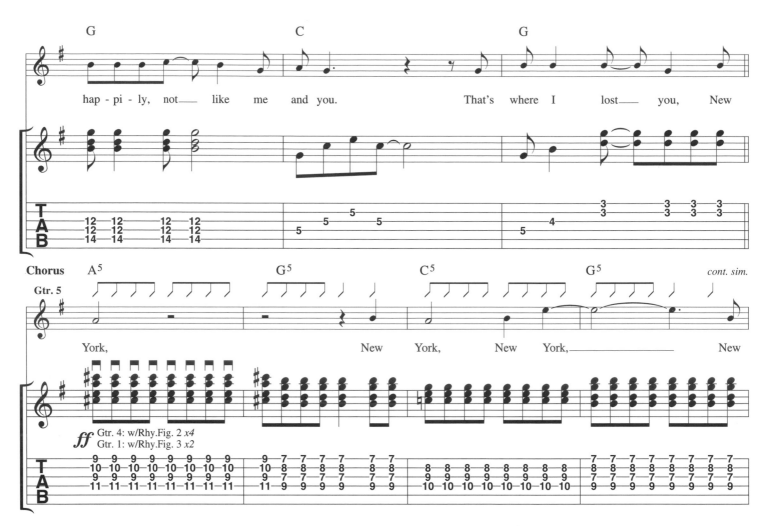

hap - pi - ly, not___ like me and you. That's where I lost___ you, New

Chorus

Gtr. 5

York, New York, New York,___ New

_ff_ Gtr. 4: w/Rhy.Fig. 2 *x4*
Gtr. 1: w/Rhy.Fig. 3 *x2*

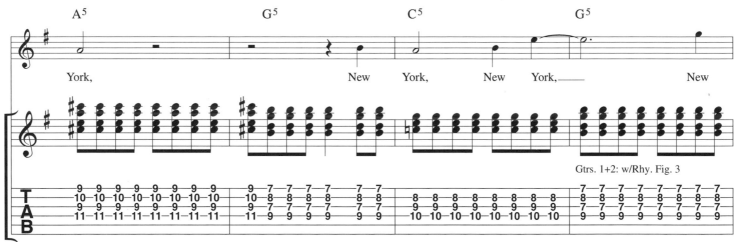

York, New York, New York,___ New

Gtrs. 1+2: w/Rhy. Fig. 3

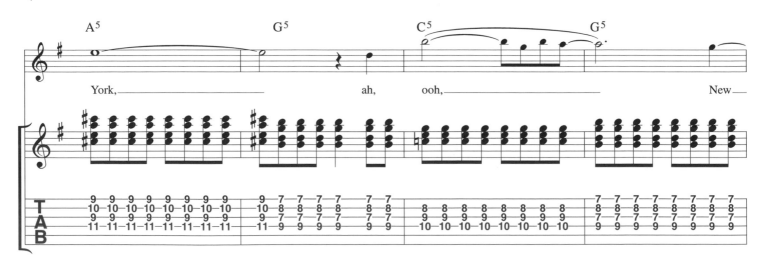

York,___ ah, ooh,___ New___

(my) mid - life cri - sis. I hit an ice - berg in my life,_____ (but you)

know I'm still a - float._____ You lose your ba - lance, lose your wife,_____

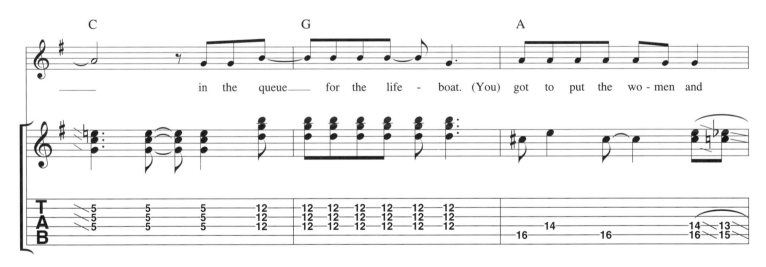

_____ in the queue_____ for the life - boat. (You) got to put the wo - men and

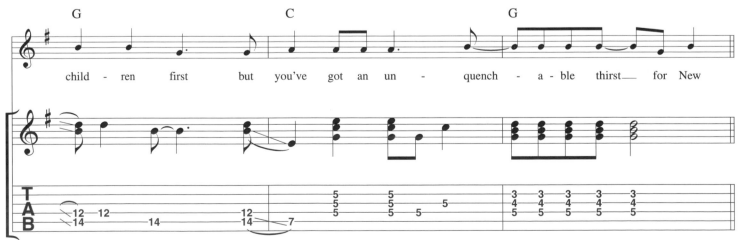

child - ren first but you've got an un - quench - a - ble thirst_____ for New

*Gtr. 3 plays with the same chord shapes as previous choruses.

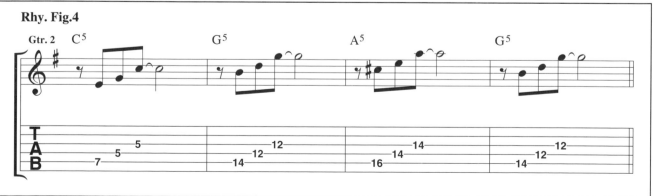

WHEN I LOOK AT THE WORLD

Music by U2
Lyrics by Bono & The Edge

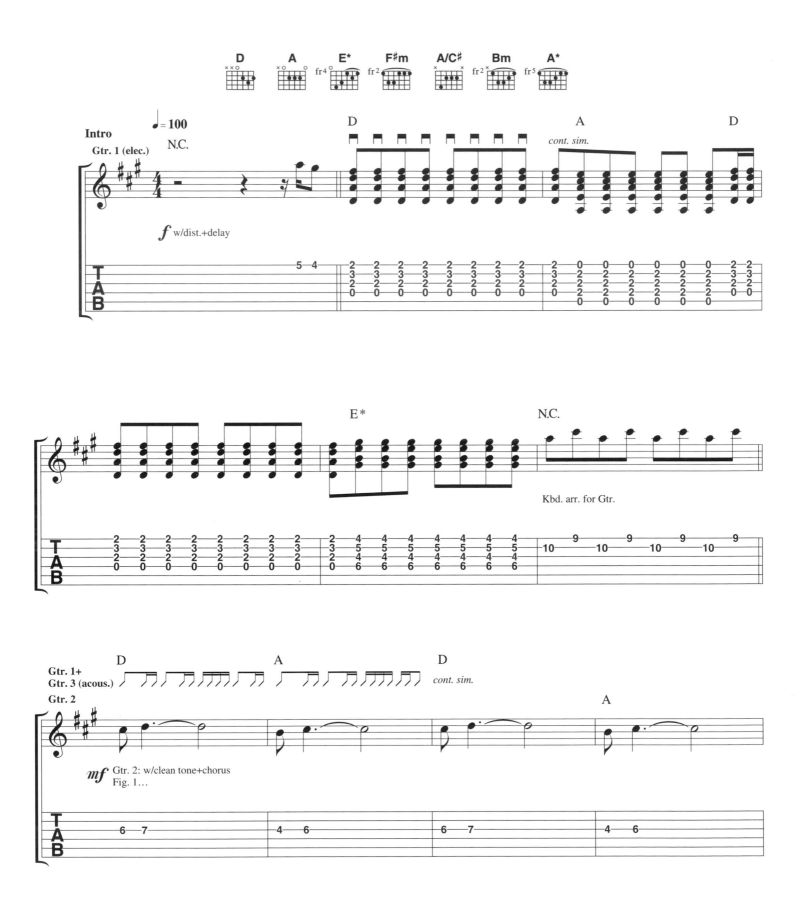

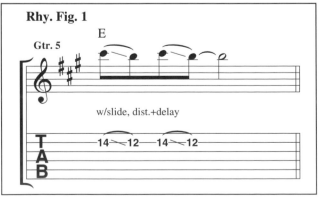

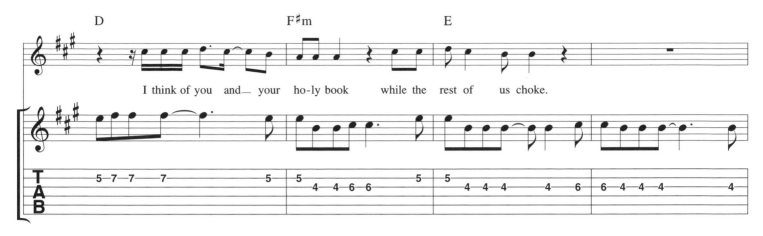

I think of you and— your ho-ly book while the rest of us choke.

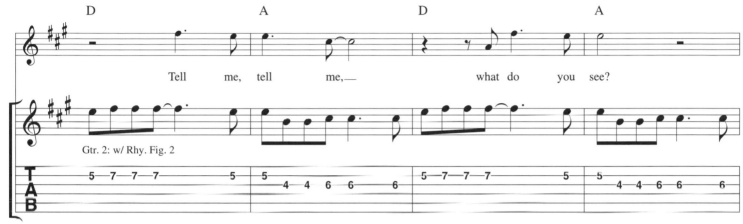

Gtr. 2: w/ Rhy. Fig. 2

Tell me, tell me,— what do you see?

Tell me, tell me,— what's wrong with me?—

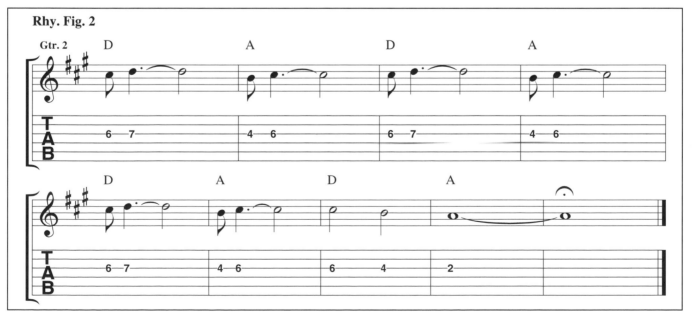

Rhy. Fig. 2

Gtr. 2

GRACE

Music by U2
Lyrics by Bono

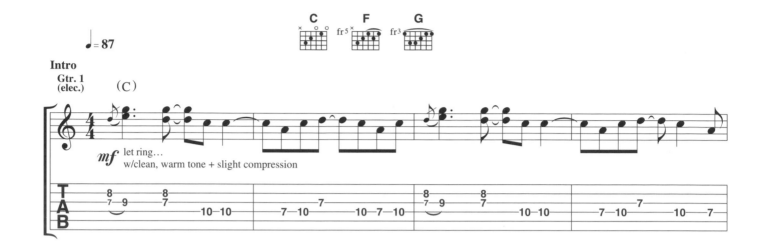

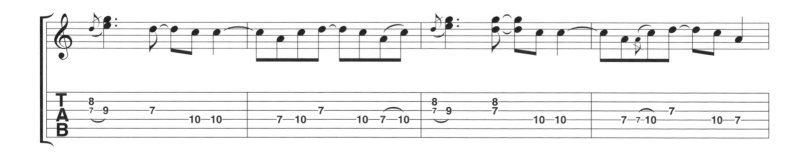

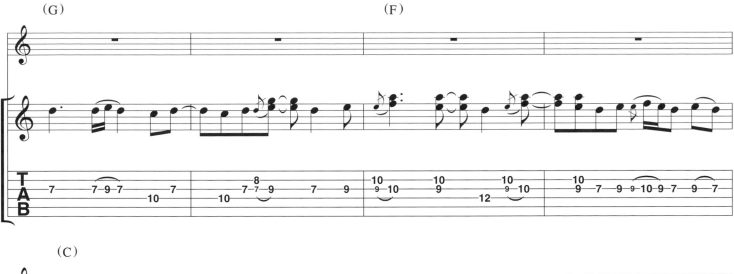

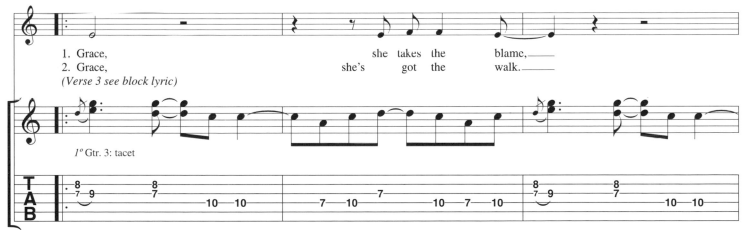

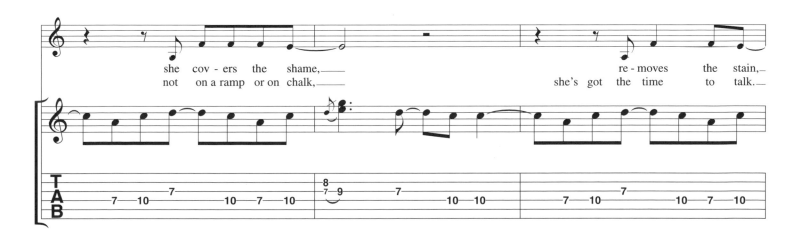

1. Grace,   she takes the   blame,____
2. Grace,   she's   got the   walk.____
(Verse 3 see block lyric)

1º Gtr. 3: tacet

she cov - ers the   shame,____   re - moves the   stain,____
not on a ramp or on chalk,____   she's got the time   to talk.____

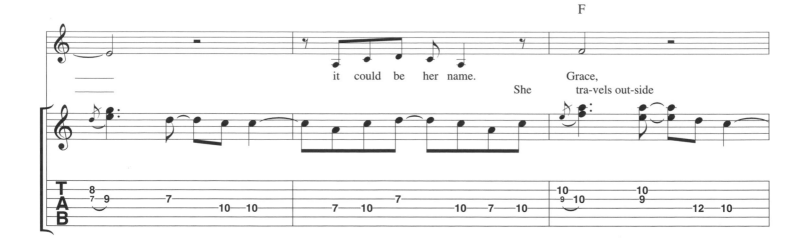

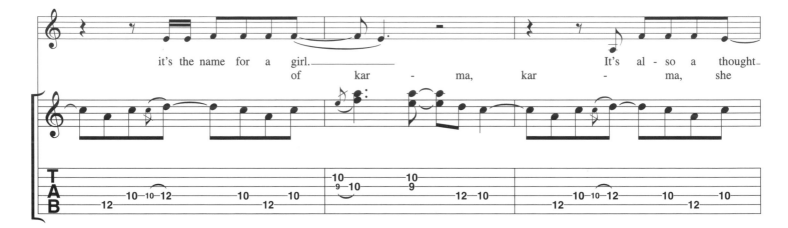

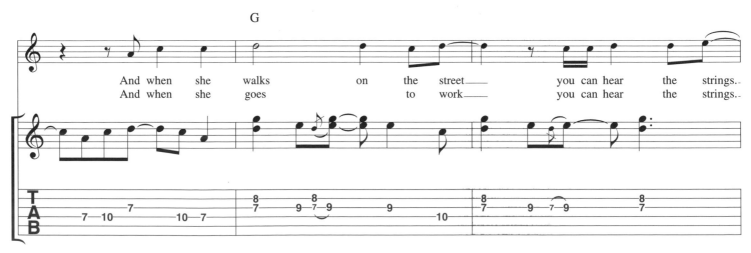

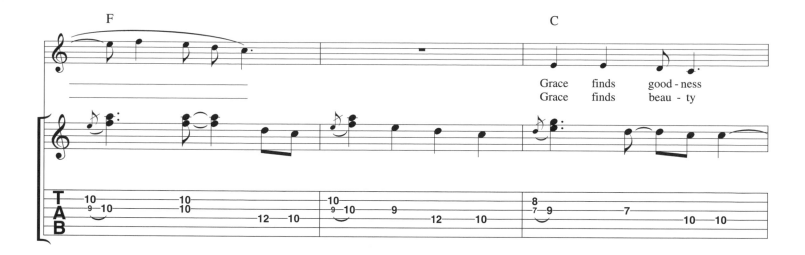

Grace   finds   good - ness
Grace   finds   beau - ty

Play 3 times

in   ev -   'ry - thing.
in   ev -   'ry - thing.

Grace finds beau - ty⎯⎯⎯   in   e - ve - ry - thing.⎯⎯

Grace finds good - ness⎯⎯⎯   in   ev - 'ry - thing.⎯⎯

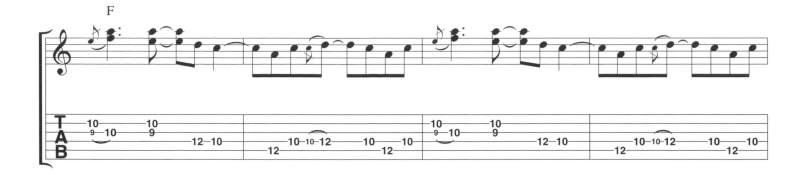

Repeat to fade

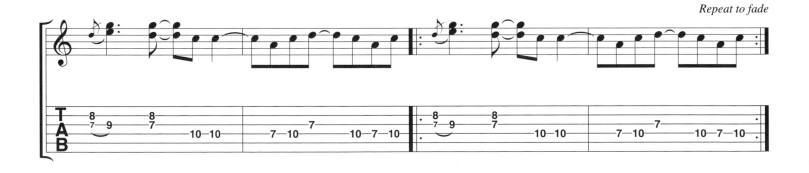

Verse 3:
Grace, she carries the world on her hips,
No champagne flute for her lips,
No twirls or skips between her finger tips.
She carries a pearl in perfect condition,
What once was hurt, what once was friction,
What left a mark no longer stings,
Because Grace makes beauty out of ugly things.

01/06 (57362)